WORLD'S
WACKIEST
ANIMALS

WORLD'S
WACKIEST
ANIMALS

CONTENTS

(AN ANIMAL WITH ★ NEXT TO ITS
NAME IS ENDANGERED OR NEARLY
ENDANGERED. AN ANIMAL WITH
★★ IS CRITICALLY ENDANGERED.
READ THE AUTHOR'S NOTE TO
LEARN MORE.)

CALIFORNIA CONDOR**

Local to North America

Believe it or not, these scavengers are bald for a reason. Their main source of nutrition is dead meat! That means these birds have to dive head-first into animal carcasses to eat. Condors can stay way cleaner without any feathers on their heads.

GHOST-FACED BAT

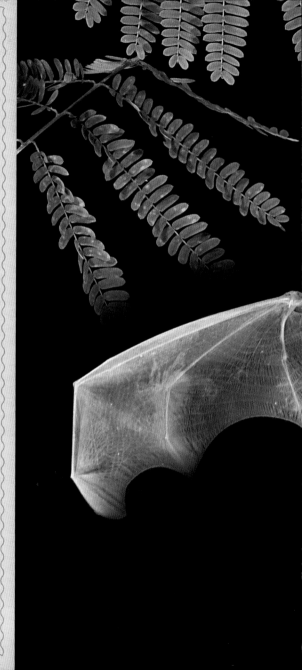

Not much is known about these elusive creatures. Most bats huddle together, but ghost-faced bats like to roost at least six inches apart. Apparently they don't like to stay too close to anyone—not even each other!

GILA MONSTER
Local to North America

Despite its scary name and venomous bite, this animal moves too slowly to be much of a threat to humans. Plus, it rarely needs to eat. By storing fat in its tail, the Gila monster can survive on as few as three meals a year!

MAGNIFICENT FRIGATEBIRD

Local to North America

Only male frigatebirds have a brilliant red throat pouch used to attract mates. But both males and females are bold in other ways. These birds feed by piracy. They chase and peck other birds until they drop or even throw up their food! Then they swoop in to steal the other bird's catch.

MEXICAN MOLE LIZARD

Local to North America

What has two arms, no legs, and looks like a snake but isn't? The Mexican mole lizard! These animals don't need legs when they've got two clawed arms perfect for burrowing underground. They spend most of their time digging in the soil for whatever critters and bugs they can munch on.

STAR-NOSED MOLE★

Local to North America

Star-nosed moles use their strange snouts for a special purpose: sniffing out food! Their nose extensions help the moles sense bugs underground as they dig. They can even smell underwater when diving in wet marshland!

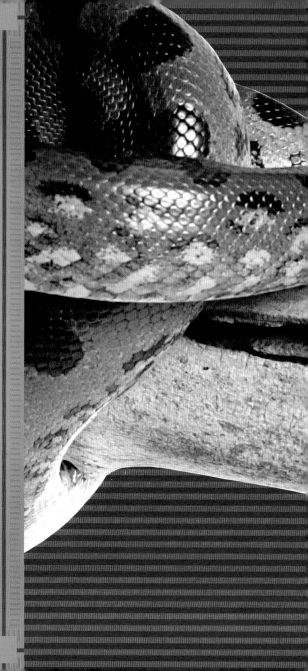

ANACONDA
Local to South America

You probably don't want to meet one of the largest snakes in the world. Anacondas weigh several hundred pounds and can sometimes grow up to 20-30 feet! They feast on large animals like capybaras, deer, and even jaguars!

ANDEAN CONDOR

Local to South America

Only male condors have the large head "comb" you see here, but both male and females share a disgusting habit: they sometimes poop directly onto their own legs. Gross! Or so you'd think. Scientists believe the liquid poop actually cleans the bird and helps cool it off.

BRAZILIAN HORNED FROG

Local to South America

This blob of a frog is tougher than it looks. It can—and will—eat anything that can fit in its mouth! Most of the time it's lizards, rodents, and other frogs. But how? These amphibians have powerful jaws. Their garbage compactor mouths crush their prey!

FLIGHTLESS CORMORANT★

Local to South America

Those little wings are mostly for decoration because cormorants can't fly! Luckily, they're much better at swimming. Flightless cormorants tuck in their tiny wings then dive deep to hunt for octopus and eels.

GALÁPAGOS TORTOISE**

Local to South America

Slow and steady wins at life. The oldest recorded Galápagos tortoise lived to 175 years old! Thanks to a slow metabolism and the ability to store a lot of water, these giants can survive up to a year without eating or drinking.

GIANT ANTEATER★

Local to South America

Are you a picky eater? Well, these mammals only eat ants! Sometimes they'll try termites, or bits of fallen fruit, but it's mostly all ants, all the time. They even have long, specialized tongues for lapping up their favorite insects. Anteaters can consume as many as 35,000 ants in one day!

GLASS FROG

Local to South America

These tiny frogs have transparent skin, so you can see their internal organs! The males of this species are super-dads who guard their eggs 24/7. They often have to kick away wasp predators that are as big as they are!

MANED WOLF
Local to South America

Is it a wolf? Is it a fox? Actually, it's neither. The maned wolf is a distinct species that lives in the savanna, where its long, deer-like legs help it see above all that tall grass!

MATAMATA TURTLE

These turtles have heads shaped like giant leaves. Their brown, boxy shells look like bark or floating wood. This helps matamata turtles blend perfectly into the leaf and plant litter at the bottom of shallow streams and pools.

34

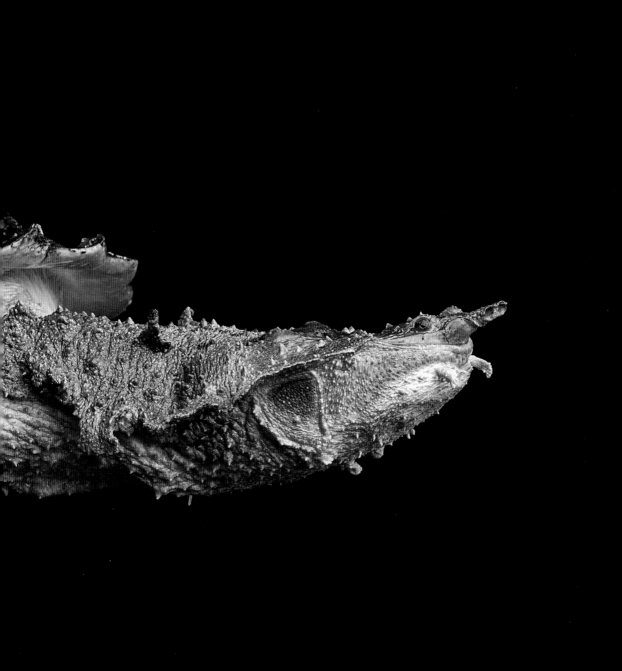

PIRANHA

Local to South America

You've probably heard of this fish's ferocious reputation. Its powerful jaws and shark-like teeth are definitely scary. But piranhas almost never attack humans or large animals. They usually scavenge on dead or dying animals. Some species are even vegetarian!

POTOO

Local to South America

These birds have cartoonishly big eyes and mouths! The better to catch big bugs with, of course. They launch off trees, swooping the insects into their gaping mouths. When they aren't hunting, potoos are hard to spot. When they are perched upright, their camouflage makes them look like tree stumps!

PYGMY MARMOSET

Local to South America

This is the world's smallest monkey! The pygmy marmoset's tail is even longer than its tiny body. It uses its long tail for balance as it dashes through forest treetops. Newborn marmosets can be as small as a human thumb!

RED-LIPPED BATFISH

Local to South America

If the red-lipped batfish's crimson kisser doesn't surprise you, the way it struts surely will. Instead of swimming, this animal walks along the ocean floor near the Galápagos Islands using its specially adapted fins.

SWORD-BILLED HUMMINGBIRD

Local to South America

En garde! Just kidding, these birds only use their extraordinarily long beaks to sip nectar or chomp on insects. Sword-billed hummingbirds take the record for the longest beaks in proportion to their bodies!

BUDAPEST PIGEON

Local to Europe

This funky bird's face was no accident. Two brothers in Budapest bred these birds to be fast in order to win pigeon races. Budapest pigeons use their bulging eyes to see far below them. They can also stay in flight for as long as five hours!

ETRUSCAN SHREW

Local to Europe

Introducing one of the world's tiniest predators! Etruscan shrews weigh less than 2 grams and could fit draped over the length of your thumb. But don't let their size fool you. These animals are skilled predators. They can eat twice their body weight in insects, all in the dark!

EURASIAN EAGLE OWL

Local to Europe

The Eurasian eagle owl has feathery ear tufts and glowing orange eyes. With a wingspan of up to 6 feet, it's one of the world's largest owls. Night vision allows this top predator to hunt in the dark for rats, rabbits, and sometimes even other birds!

HOOPOE
Local to Europe

These beautiful birds have a pretty gross defense mechanism. Baby hoopoes can turn around and squirt liquid poo at their enemies. Since it smells like rotting meat, the waste makes a powerful weapon! Hoopoes also use their sharp beaks to fend off predators.

POITOU

Local to Europe

These mop-haired animals need regular trims to stay clean, otherwise their fur becomes matted and dirty! Poitou donkeys once played an important role in breeding the best mules. Today we keep them around mostly for their pleasant company.

RED CROSSBILL

Local to Europe

You might think this bird's crossed bill gets in the way when it's trying to eat. It's the exact opposite! Red crossbills feed almost exclusively on seeds buried in the cones from trees. The beak's strange shape allows it to burrow deeply into even the trickiest pine cone.

AARDVARK

Local to Africa

This animal has a long snout to house its super-long tongue! That's because aardvarks eat lots of insects. They invade termite hills with their sticky tongues to slurp up the bugs for a delicious meal.

AFRICAN EGG-EATING SNAKE

Local to Africa

Open wide! This snake can stretch its jaws so big, it can swallow eggs whole. It doesn't have very many teeth, but uses a part of its spine to crush the eggs open and suck out the juicy bits. Then it just spits the eggshell pieces back out.

AFRICAN SHOEBILL★

Local to Africa

It's clear where this bird got its name—its beak is the same shape as the front of a shoe! The shoebill's beak is also its greatest weapon. These mighty birds use their powerful beaks to feast on lungfish, turtles, and even baby crocodiles!

AYE-AYE LEMUR★

Local to Africa

Can you hang upside down on a branch by your toes? These lemurs are experts because they spend most of their time up in the trees. They hunt for food by using their long middle fingers to tap on bark, then listening for the insects inside.

COLOBUS MONKEY

Local to Africa

The black and white Colobus monkey looks like a superhero of the forest. It has a beautiful tuft of white fur growing from its shoulders like a cape! But instead of saving the world, this primate spends most of its time hanging out in the trees, eating and relaxing.

EGYPTIAN GOOSE
Local to Africa

The Egyptian goose's entrancing eyes are surrounded by coppery coloring. But don't be fooled by its calm gaze—this bird loves aerial fights. Egyptian geese swoop at each other mid-air, and some have even attacked drones!

GALAGO

Local to Africa

These little primates have night-vision eyes! That's because galagos are mostly active after dark. They're also known as bush babies, because they spend most of their time in trees or bushes.

GERENUK

This little antelope looks a lot like a giraffe. In fact, its name means "giraffe-necked" in Somali. Gerenuks have to stand up on their hind legs to nibble on tall bushes while using their front legs to pull down high branches. They're basically always reaching for the cookie jar on the top shelf!

GREAT BLUE TURACO
Local to Africa

These striking birds may look elegant, but they are very clumsy fliers. Instead of soaring through the air, they leap from tree to tree. Great blue turacos have adapted to this setback with unique feet that can grip branches while they climb at odd angles in search of fruit.

LELWEL HARTEBEEST★

Local to Africa

The Lelwel hartebeest has a long forehead and odd V-shaped horns. It's also one of the fastest antelopes in the world. It can reach speeds over 40 miles per hour!

LONG-WATTLED UMBRELLABIRD*

Local to Africa

This bird has an adjustable beard! The feathery piece hanging from its beak is called a wattle. Only the males have wattles, and they can make them longer or shorter whenever they choose.

LOWLAND STREAKED TENREC
Local to Africa

Found only in Madagascar, these little guys use their quills for much more than defense. They actually rattle their spines at each other to communicate. Tenrec babies can develop spines in as little as 24 hours after they are born!

80

NAKED MOLE RAT

Local to Africa

This ugly burrowing rodent is sometimes called a sand puppy. Those two big front teeth aren't just for eating, they're also for digging! Naked mole rats spend most of their time underground. They can even survive as long as 18 minutes without oxygen!

PANGOLIN★★

Local to Africa

These scaly creatures are full of surprises. Pangolins don't have teeth but their powerful stomachs can grind food down into a pulp. Also, they can roll up into an armor-plated ball for self-defense!

MINUTE LEAF CHAMELEON★

Local to Africa

Quick, play dead… leaf! The minute leaf chameleon looks so much like a dead leaf it seems almost impossible for a predator to spot. These lizards are barely more than an inch long. They're one of the smallest in the world!

MOUSE LEMUR★

Local to Africa

Measuring about three and a half inches long (not counting their tails), these lemurs are one of the world's smallest primates. Mouse lemurs forage for food at night. Some people have even mistaken them for ghosts because of their large and intense eyes!

MWANZA FLAT-HEADED ROCK AGAMA

Local to Africa

It's no wonder this lizard has earned the nickname "Spider-Man Agama." Its colorful scales look just like the superhero's famous suit—and it can even climb walls! Unfortunately, these reptiles don't fight crime. They mostly just eat bugs.

SATANIC LEAF-TAILED GECKO

Local to Africa

These creatures are always watching. They never close their eyes . . . because they don't have eyelids! Instead they have transparent coverings over their eyes for protection. Satanic leaf-tailed geckos look so much like dry leaves, they're nearly impossible for predators to spot.

SPINY BUSH VIPER

Local to Africa

These venomous snakes are as prickly as they look. One bite can be fatal to humans. But don't worry, they mostly keep to themselves! Spiny bush vipers live in very remote forests and are only active at night.

BABIRUSA★

Local to Asia

Four tusks are better than two! These tusks keep growing through the babirusa's entire life, though their purpose isn't clear. Sometimes they actually start curling back toward the animal's head!

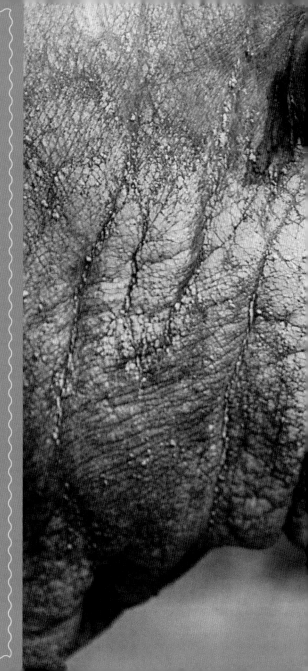

BORNEAN BEARDED PIG★

Local to Asia

These stately pigs have distinguished beards! Unlike most other pigs, Bornean bearded pigs migrate long distances, perhaps in search of food. Once a year, they form big herds with their friends and family and hit the road!

CHEVROTAIN (MOUSE DEER)★

Local to Asia

Meet the amazing mouse deer, technically neither a mouse nor a deer! Chevrotains have the cute faces of mice, but the agility of deer. And they have one secret weapon that neither animal has: fangs!

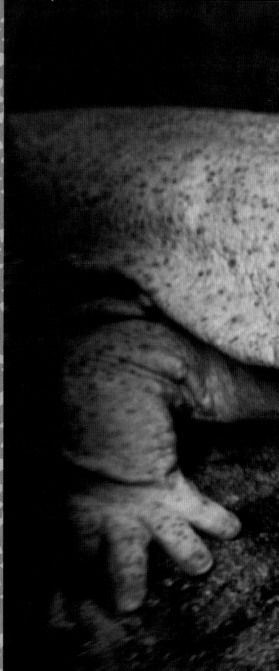

CHINESE GIANT SALAMANDER★★

Local to Asia

These slimy creatures have been around since dinosaurs roamed the Earth. They're the world's largest amphibian and can grow up to six feet long! They're also top predators, hunting for prey like worms and crayfish by sensing vibrations in the water.

CHINESE WATER DEER★

Local to Asia

Don't be fooled by these adorable deer with their long necks and big rounded ears. They're definitely not defenseless! Males have two large protruding teeth that look a lot like fangs. These cuties are not afraid to use their big chompers to defend their territory!

DAMASCUS GOAT

Local to Asia

Check out this goat's serious underbite and extra-long ears. But don't call this strange-looking animal ugly. One Damascus goat named Qahr won first prize in a famous beauty contest in Riyadh—and the competition was fierce!

GHARIAL★★

Local to Asia

Most crocodiles don't have a snout this long! With over a hundred teeth in those jaws, fish better watch out! The knobby growth at the tip of the male gharial's snout is called a ghara because it looks like a type of Indian pot of the same name.

GOBI JERBOA★

Local to Asia

These tiny rodents need extra-long socks for those giant feet! Gobi jerboa use their unusual feet not to run, but to jump. They can even leap as high as nine feet (three meters). Predators have a hard time tracking such irregular movements, so it comes in handy.

GOLDEN SNUB-NOSED MONKEY★

Local to Asia

There's a reason golden snub-nose monkeys have such flat noses: they have to survive long subzero winters in the mountains of central China. Bigger noses that expose more skin would be in danger of frostbite!

HELMETED HORNBILL**
Local to Asia

{N}ow that's a face you'll never forget. Helmeted hornbills have huge "foreheads" and striking wrinkled necks that make quite an impression. The wrinkled part of the neck is actually a pouch for carrying food!

INDIAN PURPLE FROG★

Local to Asia

Scientists only discovered these bizarre frogs in 2003, and it's no wonder why! Adult purple frogs spend most of their lives hidden underground, while the tadpoles hide on the cliffs behind waterfalls. Their tiny mouths suction onto the cliff rock, where few would ever notice them.

MARKHOR

Local to Asia

These regal creatures are the national animal of Pakistan. Only male markhors have the spiraling horns you see here. But both males and females are excellent mountain climbers! That's because they have extra wide hooves to balance over slanted and uneven terrain.

MEISHAN PIG

Local to Asia

These pigs have big droopy ears and wrinkled faces. Meishan pigs are a domesticated breed, meaning humans have managed these animals for a long time. In fact, these gentle pigs have been raised over thousands of years to be sweet and docile.

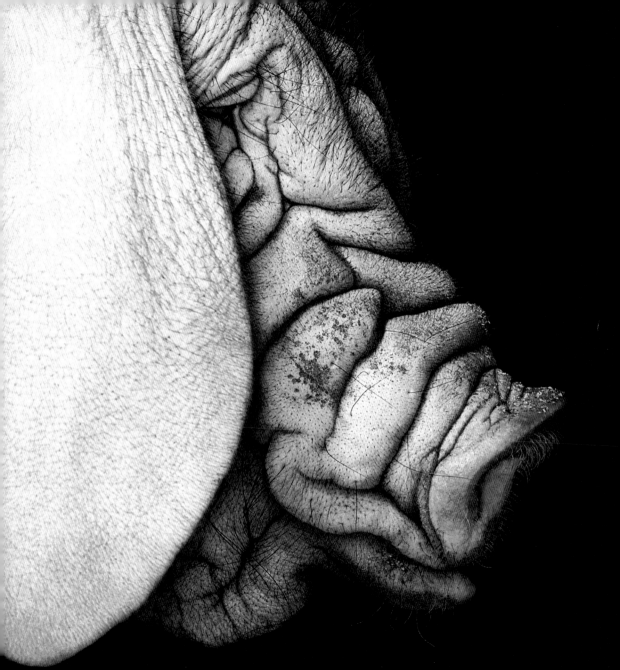

PROBOSCIS MONKEY★

Local to Asia

Only male proboscis monkeys sprout this long Pinocchio-like nose! But it's not because they tell lies. Scientists think the long nose amplifies the sound of their calls to help them compete for mates and scare away the competition.

RHINOCEROS HORNBILL★

Local to Asia

This wacky bird looks like it has a second beak growing out of its head! But the thing stacked above its beak is called a casque, and it's mostly hollow. This boosts the volume of its bird call in the forest. Make no mistake, this bird will be heard!

ROTI ISLAND SNAKE-NECKED TURTLE★★

Local to Asia

These turtles have necks so long, they can't even hide inside their shells! They have to nestle their heads in sideways. This rare species can only be found on Roti Island in Indonesia.

ROUGH-BACKED LITTER SNAKE
Local to Asia

These snakes have rows of raised scales running down their backs. They don't make for great pets, especially since they might eat your other animal friends! The rough-backed litter snake's main diet is frogs.

SHOCKING PINK DRAGON MILLIPEDE

Local to Asia

Even millipedes look pretty in pink! But beware, this bug's bright coloration is actually a warning sign to predators. Dragon millipedes are highly poisonous, and produce cyanide from their glands. Beautiful to look at, dangerous to eat!

SIAMANG★
Local to Asia

The balloon-like bulge in this primate's neck is called a throat sac. Siamangs use them to make different kinds of booming calls. When fully inflated, the throat sac can get as big as this monkey's head!

SILKWORM MOTH

Local to Asia

The silkworm moth starts out as a wormy larva called a silkworm. After it forms its cocoon, it emerges as a moth! Silkworms are special because they form cocoons with one long continuous strand. These strands can measure about 1,000 yards long!

SRI LANKA FROGMOUTH

Local to Asia

Can you imagine having a head as wide as your body? This bird feeds mostly on insects, so having a huge mouth probably helps when it's trying to catch a meal.

TARSIER MONKEY★

Local to Asia

These monkeys have eyes as big as their brains! Their eyes are so big they have to turn their whole head in order to look around. Like owls, they can actually rotate their heads nearly 180°. Creepy!

VEILED CHAMELEON

Local to Asia

Don't play hide and seek with a veiled chameleon. These tree-dwelling reptiles are masters of disguise! They can quickly change colors and patterns, using shades of red, green, yellow, orange, and blue to blend into their surroundings. They can even make themselves skinnier to look like tree branches!

CASSOWARY

Local to Australia

These birds are tougher than they look. Cassowaries have even earned the nickname "murderbird," because they are fast and armed with a five-inch claw on each foot. You do not want to be on the other side of this hundred-pound bird's kick!

SHORT-BEAKED ECHIDNA

Local to Australia

The short-beaked echidna is a monotreme, a type of mammal that lays eggs. A baby echidna, called a puggle, spends the first three months of its life inside its mother's pouch. When the puggle gets prickly, the mother makes it move out!

FRILLED DRAGON

Local to Australia

These lizards are all frills and no fight! When they flare their neck flaps, open their mouths, and hiss, it means they're scared. They're trying to intimidate predators. If that doesn't work, they totally turn tail and run for the nearest tree!

LAUGHING KOOKABURRA

Local to Australia

The kookaburra has a kooky bird call. It sounds like the bird is laughing hysterically! It's almost contagious. Unfortunately, they do like to start up their cackling at the crack of dawn. That's not funny at all if you're trying to sleep nearby!

MARY RIVER TURTLE★

Local to Australia

The Mary River turtle can stay submerged for as long as three days without surfacing! When underwater, it exchanges oxygen and carbon dioxide by putting its bum in the air and breathing through the opening there!

PIG-NOSED TURTLE★

Local to Australia

Turtles need to be sneaky when they poke their heads out of the water to breathe. Why? To hide from predators! And pig-nosed turtles are masters at this. They stick out just the very tips of their noses and keep the rest of their bodies submerged underwater.

PLATYPUS
Local to Australia

Check out the Frankenstein of animals. This mammal has the bill of a duck, the body of an otter, and the tail of a beaver. Male platypuses even have . . . toxic feet? Small spurs on their feet contain venom that these animals can use for self defense.

SUPERB BIRD OF PARADISE

Local to Australia

Love changes a person—or a bird. These birds look quite ordinary on a normal day. But when a male is trying to win over a female, he totally transforms. The black feathers on his back pop up to form a cape, and its bright blue breast feathers spring outward like a fan.

VICTORIA CROWNED PIGEON

Local to Australia

This beautiful bird certainly looks regal. A "crown" of lace-like feathers grows out of its head. Victoria crowned pigeons are almost as big as turkeys, and spend most of their time on the ground. The males even bow to females when they are courting. How elegant!

SOUTHERN ELEPHANT SEAL★

Local to New Zealand

Can you guess why they're named elephant seals? It's because of their long trunk-like noses, though only males have this distinguishing characteristic. These enormous animals dive underwater to hunt for fish and squid. And they can stay under for as long as two hours!

CHINSTRAP PENGUIN

Local to the Antarctic

These birds look like they are wearing little swimming caps, which is fitting for animals that spend so much time taking dips into the sea. Chinstrap penguins are named after the thin marking below their beaks. These penguins usually spend less than a minute underwater where they hunt for fish and krill.

NARWHAL

Local to the Arctic

Meet the "unicorns of the sea." Their special tusks can grow as long as 8-9 feet. Scientists' best guess is that narwhals use their tusks to stun fish as they hunt. The long tusk may also be part of a male's appeal in mating rituals.

ATLANTIC PUFFIN★

Local to the Arctic

How many fish do you think a puffin can hold in its beak? One puffin in Britain was found with 62 fish in its mouth! These extremely talented birds can dive underwater for as long as a minute and fly up to 55 miles per hour.

ANGLERFISH
Found in Worldwide Oceans

Anglerfish live in the deepest, darkest part of the ocean. Female anglers have a "fishing rod" on their heads, with a light on the end. They use these rods to lure their prey directly into their mouths.

BASKING SHARK★

Found in Worldwide Oceans

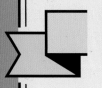 pen wide! Basking sharks feed by opening their jaws and exposing the gills inside. They use these gills to filter tiny zooplankton from the water. Basking sharks can filter up to 2,000 tons of seawater per hour! Best of all, they are no danger at all to humans.

BLACK DRAGONFISH

Found in Worldwide Oceans

These deep-sea creatures practically invented stealth mode. They hunt in the absolute darkness of ocean depths where it's important to remain completely invisible. Black dragonfish have skin that actually absorbs light!

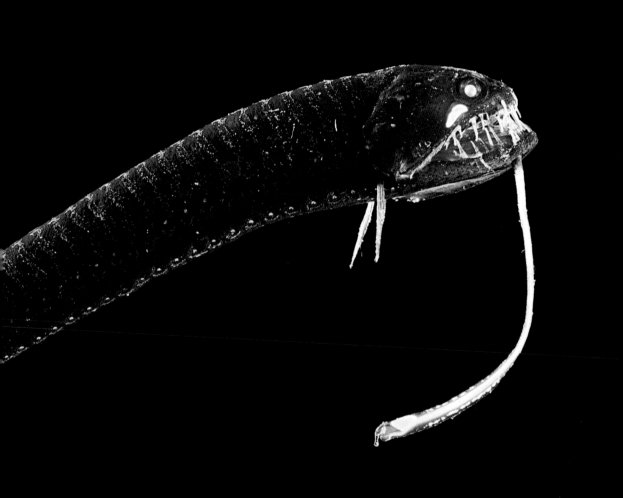

CORAL
Found in Worldwide Oceans

That's right—these rock-like, plant-looking things are actually classified as animals! They're made up of thousands of tiny polyps. These polyps build a hard exterior to protect their soft inner bodies. So what you think of as coral is actually polyp skeleton!

CROWN-OF-THORNS STARFISH

Found in Indian and Pacific Oceans

These huge spiny starfish actually pose a pretty big threat to coral reefs. They feed on coral by turning their stomachs inside out—through their mouths! Then they digest the nutrients directly off the coral itself.

GIANT CLAM★

Found in Indian and Pacific Oceans

Have you ever picked up a shell as big as this one? Giant clams look like bright, beautiful frills that grow on coral rock. Some can grow as long as four feet! These gentle giants have a fictional reputation as "maneaters." They actually mostly eat the nutrients from plankton and algae.

GLAUCUS ATLANTICUS

Found in Worldwide Oceans

These sea slugs also go by another name: blue dragons. Unlike dragons, the glaucus atlanticus is barely an inch long. But make no mistake, these tiny creatures pack a punch. They absorb the poison from venomous prey and store it as a defense mechanism.

HAIRY FROGFISH

Found in Worldwide Oceans

The "hairs" you see on hairy frogfish are actually flexible spines! They help the animal blend into the coral and seaweed of its habitat. It has one really long spine that looks like a worm—perfect for luring fish when it's snack time!

IMMORTAL JELLYFISH

Found in Worldwide Oceans

Can immortal jellyfish really live forever? These jellyfish have a unique trick for when they're injured or starving. They can change back to their infant forms! They age backward until they're polyps again.

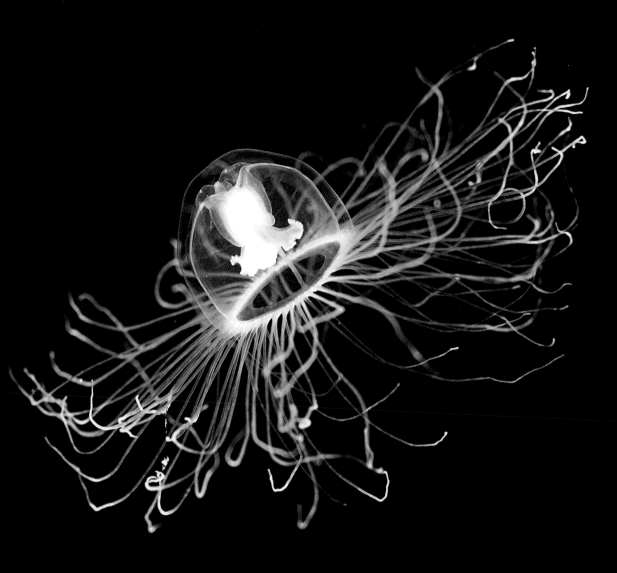

LANTERNFISH

Found in Worldwide Oceans

How do you get around in the dark? Lanternfish live in deep seas, far past where light can penetrate the ocean. So they carry around some flashlights! Tiny light-producing organs called photophores line this creature's belly and nose.

MANDARIN-FISH

These fish are as beautiful as they are smelly! Mandarinfish don't have scales. They must protect themselves with a putrid, toxic slime over their skin instead. If the distinctive stench doesn't warn predators away, tiny spines inject toxic mucus into anything that touches this stunning stinker.

MANTIS SHRIMP

Found in Worldwide Oceans

A mantis shrimp can deliver a fatal blow in a fraction of a second. Its hinged arms fold away under its head, then dart out in a movement so quick it can only be caught on super high-speed camera.

MIMIC OCTOPUS

Found in Indian and Pacific Oceans

Have you ever pretended to be someone else? These marine "shapeshifters" can imitate not just one, but several different animals! Mimic octopuses can pretend to be lionfish, jellyfish, or sea snakes. By pretending to be a predator, they can frighten off their enemies. It's how they stay safe!

MORAY EEL

These eerie hunters lie in wait in the holes of coral reefs. You might see them slowly opening and closing their mouths. They may look hungry and threatening, but moray eels actually move their mouths in order to breathe! The motion brings more water to pass through their gills.

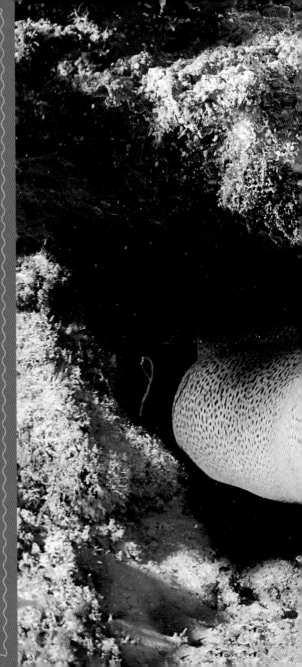

OCEAN SUNFISH★

Found in Worldwide Oceans

These frisbee-shaped fish aren't particularly good swimmers, but they still manage to surf the ocean at a leisurely pace. Ocean sunfish are huge. They're the heaviest of bony fish, and can grow as long as 14 feet!

RED LIONFISH

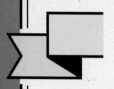

Found in Worldwide Oceans

Those showy spines look beautiful to humans, but dangerous to other fish. They're a defense mechanism that tells ocean predators "Don't eat me!" Red lionfish don't use their spines to hunt. Instead, they slowly stalk prey until they get close enough to suction it into their mouths.

WEEDY SEADRAGON

Found in Pacific Ocean

Is that seaweed or a seahorse? It's a weedy seadragon! These animals often just go with the flow of ocean currents, so they're easy to mistake for floating seaweed. Like seahorses, the males of this species are the ones to give birth! The weedy seadragon hides the fertilized eggs on the underside of his tail.

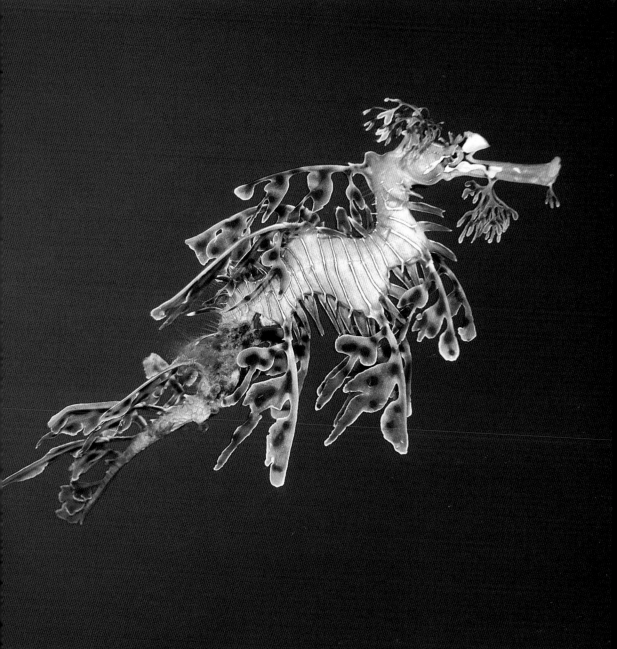

WHITEMARGIN STARGAZER

Found in Indian and Pacific Oceans

*D*id the ocean floor just grow a...face? Whitemargin stargazers blend in so well with sand, they're practically part of the ocean floor! Their eyes sit on top of their heads, always searching for food. They even have worm-like lures near their mouths to draw their prey near.

TARDIGRADE

Found in Worldwide Waters

These near-microscopic creatures are practically invincible! They can live under the crushing pressure of the deepest part of the ocean, and even withstand the burning radiation of outer space!

AUTHOR'S NOTE

Every animal in this book with a ★ next to its name is vulnerable to becoming endangered or is already endangered. Animals with ★ ★ are critically endangered. Endangered animals may soon become extinct. The numbers of these animals are decreasing, mostly due to pollution, habitat loss, overhunting and overfishing, or climate change. All of these environmental problems have been caused by humans.

But there are ways you can help. Visit the websites below to learn more about how you can get involved.

WORLD WILDLIFE FUND
worldwildlife.org

NATURAL RESOURCES DEFENSE COUNCIL
nrdc.org

WILDLIFE CONSERVATION SOCIETY
wcs.org

RAINFOREST ACTION NETWORK
ran.org

NATURE CONSERVANCY
nature.org

PHOTO CREDITS

Cover: SensorSpot/Getty Images (veiled chameleon); National Geographic Image Collection/Alamy (naked mole rat); Craig Ansibin/Shutterstock (helmeted hornbill); Floridapfe from S.Korea Kim in cherl/Getty Images (fennec fox) / **3:** National Geographic Image Collection/Alamy / **4-5 (and throughout):** Popmarleo/Getty Images (pattern) / **7:** Justin Hofman/Alamy / **8-9:** SuperStock / Alamy / **10 (and throughout):** miakievy/Getty Images (pattern) / **11:** Credit: Nature Picture Library / Alamy Stock Photo12 (and throughout): milezaway/Shutterstock (pattern) / **13:** Matt Cornish/Shutterstock / **15:** Chris Mattison/Alamy / **17:** Agnieszka Bacal/Shutterstock / **18-19:** petographer/Alamy / **21:** reisegraf.ch/Shutterstock / **23:** Danita Delimont/Alamy / **25:** Guido Vermeulen-Perdaen/Shutterstock / **27:** Marc Shandro/Getty Images / **29:** esdeem/Shutterstock / **31:** Dr Morley Read/Shutterstock / **33:** Ger Bosma/Getty Images / **34-35:** Seregraff/Shutterstock / **37:** Martin Shields/Alamy / **39:** Martin Mecnarowski/Shutterstock / **41:** Edwin Butter/Shutterstock / **42-43:** Mark Conlin/Alamy / **45:** Mark Thomas/Alamy / **47:** Eric Isselee/Shutterstock / **49:** Thailand Wildlife/Alamy / **51:** Lemtal Sergei/Shutterstock / **53:** Piotr Krzeslak/Shutterstock / **55:** dmaroscar/Getty Images / **57:** Bob Pool/Shutterstock / **59:** Cultura Creative Ltd/Alamy / **61:** Helmut Gothel Symbiosis/Alamy / **63:** imageBROKER/Alamy / **65:** imageBROKER/Alamy / **67:** Nagel Photography/Shutterstock / **69:** imageBROKER/Alamy / **71:** Mark Sheridan-Johnson/Shutterstock / **73:** Ihab Henri/Shutterstock / **75:** Serguei Koultchitskii/Shutterstock / **77:** SoopySue/Getty Images / **78-79:** Juan Jose Arango/VWPics/Alamy / **81:** Arto Hakola/Getty Images / **83:** National Geographic Image Collection/Alamy / **85:** imageBROKER/Alamy / **86-87:** blickwinkel/Alamy / **89:** Hajakely/Shutterstock / **91:** Cat Downie/Shutterstock / **93:** Valt Ahyppo/Shutterstock / **95:** Mark_Kostich/Shutterstock / **96-97:** MANOJ SHAH/Getty Images / **99:** Vladimir Wrangel/Shutterstock / **101:** teekayu/Shutterstock / **102-103:** Best View Stock/Getty Images / **105:** Simon Litten/Alamy / **107:** Trofimov Denis/Shutterstock / **108-109:** sylvain cordier/Getty Images / **111:** Nature Picture Library/Alamy / **113:** V_E/Shutterstock / **115:** Craig Ansibin/Shutterstock / **117:** Hornbil Images/Alamy Stock Photo / **119:** blickwinkel/Alamy Stock Photo / **121:** Tim Flach/Getty Images / **123:** Yusnizam Yusof/Shutterstock / **125:** aiman_zhafransyah/Shutterstock / **126-127:** Mark Newman/Getty Images / **129:** reptiles4all/Shutterstock / **130-131:** Thailand Wildlife/Alamy / **132-133:** Zoonar GmbH/Alamy / **135:** Amadeu_Ito/Shutterstock / **137:** Albert Wright/iStockphoto/Getty Images / **139:** Don Mammoser/Shutterstock / **141:** Daniel Rochelle/Getty Images / **143:** Dave Watts/Alamy / **145:** Jarrod Calati/Shutterstock / **147:** PetlinDmitry/Shutterstock / **149:** Ken Griffiths/Shutterstock / **150-151:** RobertDowner/iStockphoto/Getty Images / **153:** daniilphotos/Shutterstock / **155:** Dave Watts/Alamy / **157:** Gabbro/Alamy / **159:** Frank Cornelissen/Shutterstock / **161:** worldswildlifewonders/Shutterstock / **163:** nis vanarin/Shutterstock / **165:** Dave Fleetham/Perspectives/Getty Images / **167:** Rudmer Zwerver/Shutterstock / **169:** Doug Perrine/Alamy / **171:** Dan Burton/Nature Picture Library/Getty Images / **173:** Solvin Zankl/Alamy / **175:** Humberto Ramirez/Getty Images / **177:** Richard Whitcombe/Shutterstock / **179:** imageBROKER/Alamy / **181:** S.Rohrlach/Shutterstock / **183:** Ye Choh Wah/Shutterstock / **185:** zaferkizilkaya/Shutterstock / **187:** Solvin Zankl/Alamy / **188-189:** Jack Foto Focus/Shutterstock / **190-191:** JoramZ/Shutterstock / **193:** stephan kerkhofs/Shutterstock / **194-195:** Rich Carey/Shutterstock / **197:** WaterFrame/Alamy / **199:** Dennis attard/Shutterstock / **201:** Stephen Frink Collection/Alamy / **202-203:** Ethan Daniels/Shutterstock / **204-205:** Sebastian Kaulitzki/Shutterstock

ACKNOWLEDGMENTS

Publishing Director: Piers Pickard / **Publisher:** Hanna Otero / **Editor:** Rhoda Belleza / **Author:** Anna Poon / **Art Director:** Ryan Thomann / **Designer:** Dave Kopka / **Print Production:** Lisa Ford

Published in February 2020 by Lonely Planet Global Limited
CRN: 554153
ISBN: 978-1-78868-757-7
www.lonelyplanetkids.com
© Lonely Planet 2020

Printed in China
10 9 8 7 6 5 4 3 2 1

STAY IN TOUCH - lonelyplanet.com/contact

Lonely Planet Offices:

AUSTRALIA The Malt Store, Level 3, 551 Swanston St, Carlton, Victoria 3053   T: 03 8379 8000

IRELAND Digital Depot, Roe Lane (off Thomas St), Digital Hub, Dublin 8, D08 TCV4, Ireland

USA 155 Filbert St., Ste. 208, Oakland, CA 94607 T: 510 250 6400

UK 240 Blackfriars Rd, London SE1 8NW T: 020 3771 5100